THE STORY BEHIND

SILK

Ann Weil

www.raintreepublishers.co.uk
Visit our website to find out more information about Raintree books.

To order:
☎ Phone 0845 6044371
🖷 Fax +44 (0) 1865 312263
🖳 Email myorders@raintreepublishers.co.uk

Customers from outside the UK please telephone +44 1865 312262

Raintree is an imprint of Capstone Global Library Limited, a company incorporated in England and Wales having its registered office at 7 Pilgrim Street, London, EC4V 6LB – Registered company number: 6695582

Text © Capstone Global Library Limited 2012
First published in hardback in 2012
The moral rights of the proprietor have been asserted

Edited by Megan Cotugno and Diyan Leake
Designed by Philippa Jenkins
Original illustrations © Capstone Global
    Library Ltd (2012)
Illustrated by David Westerfield
Picture research by Hannah Taylor and Mica Brancic
Originated by Capstone Global Library Ltd
Printed and bound in China by CTPS

ISBN 978 1 406 22927 1 (hardback)
15 14 13 12 11
10 9 8 7 6 5 4 3 2 1

British Library Cataloguing in Publication Data
Weil, Ann.
The story behind silk. – (True stories)
677.3'9-dc22
A full catalogue record for this book is available from the British Library.

Acknowledgements
We would like to thank the following for permission to reproduce photographs: Alamy pp. **4** (© Robert Harding Picture Library Ltd), **22**, **24 left** (© World History Archive); Ancient Art & Architecture p. **6** (Uniphoto); The Art Archive p. **7** (Victoria and Albert Museum London/Eileen Tweedy); Corbis pp. **13** (Bettmann), **20** (Massimo Listri), **21** (Olix Wirtinger); Getty Images pp **11** (MPI), **24 right** (Keystone-France/Gamma-Keystone); iStockphoto pp. **17** (© Terraxplorer), **27** (© Amber Plank); Photolibrary pp. **8** (De Agostini Editore/A Dagli Orti), **16** (Imagebroker.net/Gerhard Zwerger-Schoner), **15 bottom** (Peter Arnold); Science Photo Library p. **14 top** (E. R. Degginger); Shutterstock pp. **iii** (© Holbox), **5** (© Tonobalaguerf), **15 right** (© Gelinshu), **18** (© Anyka), **19** (© Stanislav Komogorov), **23** (© Christopher Waters), **25** (© Anka Kaczmarzyk) **26** (© Subbotina Anna).

Cover photograph of ties on the shelf of a shop in the Como region, Italy reproduced with permission of Shutterstock (© Alexander Chaikin).

We would like to thank Ann Fullick for her invaluable help in the preparation of this book.

Every effort has been made to contact copyright holders of material reproduced in this book. Any omissions will be rectified in subsequent printings if notice is given to the publisher.

Contents

Some words are shown in bold, **like this**. You can find out what they mean by looking in the glossary on page 30.

Amazing silk

▲ People sell silk fabrics in markets, such as this one in China.

Silk is the original **luxury** fabric. From its beginnings in ancient China to modern times, silk has been the choice for people who could afford the best. People preferred it to other fabrics such as cotton and wool. Silk feels smoother and lighter. It is prettier. Some silk fabrics shimmer like precious jewels. This is because every silk **fibre** is shaped like a triangle. Silk acts like a **prism** that reflects light in a special way.

Silk can keep people warmer when it is cold outside and cooler when it is hot. Silk fabric does not crease like other cloth, so it looks neater. Another amazing thing about silk is how little it has changed since its discovery thousands of years ago. Silk is still made only by the caterpillar of a particular kind of moth. These insects are called silkworms.

What's in a name?

The scientific name for silkworms is *Bombyx mori*. That means "silkmoth of the mulberry tree".

◀ Silkworm caterpillars feed on the leaves of mulberry trees.

The silk goddess

According to legend, the Chinese emperor Huang Di was the first ruler to wear a silk robe.

Travel back 5,000 years to ancient China ... a time before histories were written down, when the Chinese people thought their emperor was part god. **Legends** tell how the young wife of the first emperor discovered silk. The teenage empress was sitting in the shade of a mulberry tree, drinking tea, when a silkworm **cocoon** fell from a branch into her cup! She watched as the hot tea dissolved some of the sticky stuff that held the cocoon together. A single silk **fibre** began to unwind. This gave the empress a wonderful idea.

She had her ladies-in-waiting gather more cocoons. They put these in hot water and made thread from the fibres. Then the clever empress made a **loom** and used it to weave the thread into a fine cloth. She **embroidered** the cloth and made it into a robe for her husband. It was by far the most beautiful piece of clothing the emperor had ever seen.

The empress continued to work with silk. She studied the silkworms. She showed her ladies-in-waiting how to gather cocoons, make silk thread, and weave it into cloth. She became known as the Goddess of Silk. We may never know if this legend is fact or fiction – or a mixture of both. No matter how it happened, the discovery of silk changed China and the world!

▼ **This Chinese drawing was done in the 1600s. It shows people making silk at home.**

The secret of silk

▲ This Chinese silk embroidery is from the 1800s. The elephant has been a symbol of power and wisdom since ancient times.

At first, only the Chinese royal family wore silk clothing. Emperors gave silk away as gifts and rewards. People began making silk throughout China. But they did not give away the secret of its source: silkworms. Even people who saw and used this amazing fabric had no idea it was made by **domesticated** insects. The Chinese guarded this secret for more than 2,000 years. It was the best-kept secret in history.

Silk became extremely valuable, and the Chinese were the only people who knew how to make it. Making silk became a well-organized **cottage industry** in China. Families, including young children, worked together from their homes to produce silk. They used silk like money, even for paying their **taxes**.

Keeping control of silk production made the Chinese royal family even richer and more powerful. To protect their interests, they made it against the law to reveal the secret of silk to an outsider. The punishment was death!

Not for everyone

There were strict rules in ancient China about who could wear silk. Of course the royal family had the best silk clothing. Some high-ranking people in the government were allowed to wear clothes made from silk. **Scholars** could wear silk, too. But wealthy merchants who made their living by trading silk were forbidden to wear what they sold.

Chinese silk in ancient Egypt

Silk from China was found in the hair of an Egyptian mummy from 1070 BC. This is the earliest date for which we have proof of a silk trade.

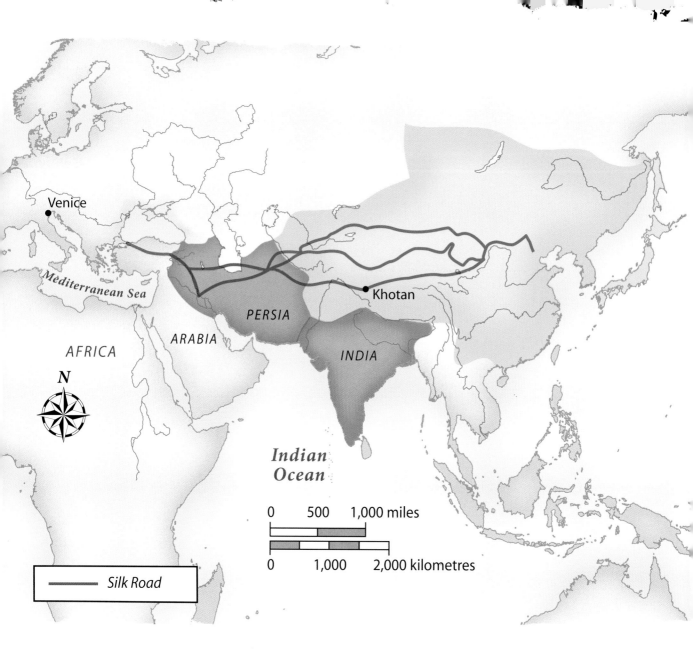

The Silk Road

The Silk Road was a system of **caravan** routes. It was 6,500 kilometres (4,000 miles) long. These routes led through China and the mountains and deserts of Asia. Traders began travelling the Silk Road around 200 BC.

Silk was one of the main goods traded from East to West. Jade, paper, spices, horses, and even grapes were also traded. Traders stopped at towns to rest and water their animals. They traded stories as well as goods.

New knowledge, ideas, and religious beliefs travelled along the Silk Road. China was no longer isolated, but it was still very difficult and dangerous to get to and from the birthplace of silk.

The secret is out!

Raising silkworms to make silk is called **sericulture**. By around AD 300, sericulture was spreading from China to other parts of Asia. People in in India, Japan, Korea, and Persia (now called Iran) began raising silkworms. Still, these Asian countries kept the secret of silk from people in the west.

The princess with silkworms in her hair

A well-known **legend** tells how a Chinese princess hid silkworms in her fancy hairdo so she could take them with her when she left home to marry an Indian prince of Khotan. Khotan became famous for its silks. If this story is true, it could explain how the secret of silk spread to India.

▼ This detail from a larger illustrated map shows Marco Polo (see pages 12–13) and his fellow travellers on the Silk Road.

Silk and the Romans

The Romans traded huge amounts of gold for silk. Still, they knew almost nothing about China, its people, or how silk was made. They had no idea it came from worms. They thought silk grew on Chinese trees!

People and news did not travel long distances in ancient times. Even traders did not travel the entire Silk Road. It was more like a relay race. Each trader travelled only part of the total distance. Goods were exchanged at each stop and the price increased each time!

The Roman emperor feared that his people's desire for silk was costing them too much money. The solution to paying so much for silk was to learn how to make it. Finally, around AD 550, Emperor Justinian got silkworm eggs and mulberry seeds from travelling monks who had smuggled them from Asia. The **Roman Empire** became a new centre of silk production, and **sericulture** began to spread throughout western Asia and Europe.

Marco Polo (1254–1324)

Marco Polo travelled the Silk Road from his home in Venice, Italy. Historians think he may have stayed in China for more than 20 years. After his return to Italy, he told people what he has seen. A book called *Travels of Marco Polo* finally gave people in Europe a real look at the wealth and culture of the Chinese Empire.

▲ Marco Polo travelled to China as a
young man. He spent his old age
back in Italy.

The life cycle of a silkworm

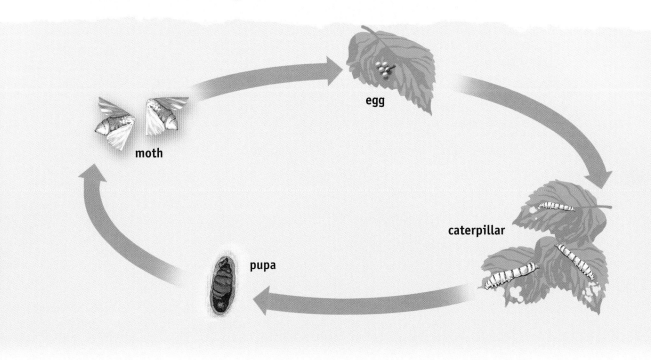

egg

moth

caterpillar

pupa

▲ It all starts with an egg the size of a pin.

Silk is a natural **fibre**, produced by an insect called a silkworm. Silkworms aren't really worms at all. Silkworms are caterpillars, a stage of the life cycle of a particular kind of moth. When they are about to turn into a moth, they spin a **cocoon** made of **raw silk**.

Raising silkworms takes time, but each step is simple enough for even young children to do. The tiny eggs need warmth to hatch. Traditionally, Chinese women "wore" the eggs in small bags close to their body. Their body heat encouraged the eggs to hatch.

Food, glorious food!

The tiny caterpillars come out hungry and begin eating. They eat only one kind of food: fresh mulberry leaves. But they eat a lot! They eat constantly, night and day. Their munching sounds like rain pattering against a roof. They grow and moult (shed their skin) four times. In a month, their weight increases 10,000 times!

As it grows, the silkworm makes a jelly-like substance inside its silk **glands**. This is what it uses to spin its **cocoon**. The gooey liquid hardens when it comes in contact with the air.

It takes a silkworm about three days to spin its cocoon. The cocoon is actually a single fibre. Some can be over 1 kilometre (half a mile) long! As the silkworm makes its cocoon, it becomes a **pupa**. Inside its cocoon, the pupa changes completely from a crawling caterpillar to a moth with wings.

◀ Silkworm eggs can hatch in about 10 days.

▼ Silkworm cocoons are white or yellow.

◀ When the silkworm is fully grown, it is ready to spin its cocoon.

From cocoon to cloth

In the wild, the moth would spit out a liquid that
dissolves part of its **cocoon**, allowing it to break
out of its case. But this would damage the single
silk **fibre**.

Most cocoons are heated to kill the insect inside before it breaks out of its cocoon. This is called stifling. A few silkworms are allowed to complete their life cycle to produce eggs, which are needed to continue the supply of silkworms. One female moth can lay as many as 500 eggs!

Cocoons are still placed in hot water and unwound in pretty much the same way they were thousands of years ago in ancient China. The fibres from several cocoons are twisted together to make a single thread of silk. This is wound onto a **spool**. Threads may be wound together again to make stronger, thicker threads. It takes 30,000 to 40,000 silkworms to produce just 5.5 kilograms (12 pounds) of **raw silk**. Then the raw silk is woven into cloth. Some people still weave silk by hand using traditional **looms**. However, most silk cloth is made using machines.

Wild silk

Some people do not like the idea that silkworms are killed to make fabric for their clothes. But they can still wear wild silk. Wild silk, which is also called tussah, is made from broken cocoons after the moth comes out.

▼ People still make fine-looking silk fabrics the old-fashioned way, using ancient looms like this one.

Silk around the world

▲ This bride chose a dazzling red silk gown for her wedding day.

As more countries produced their own silk, the price dropped. Silk was still a **luxury** fabric. But it was a luxury more and more people could afford.

Silk in Asia

Sericulture is still a **cottage industry** in much of Asia. Families work together at home, raising silkworms to make money. Although silk itself is a luxury product, looking after the silkworms is not so glamorous or difficult.

India is the second largest silk producer (after China), and uses more silk than any other country. Indian women wear silk **saris**. Silk is also the choice for men's and women's wedding clothes.

Silk made in Thailand is well known for its quality, beauty, colour, and design. Women in the north-east part of the country raise mulberry trees and silkworms in almost the same way that people did centuries ago. They pluck **cocoons** from the trees, spin and dye the thread, and weave it into fabric to be sold overseas.

You can't make a silk purse out of a sow's ear

This is a saying that means you can't make something good or useful from bad or wrong materials, or you can't turn something ugly into a beautiful object.

▼ People in Asia make snack foods from silkworm **pupae**. Koreans boil pupae with spices and seasonings. In China, street vendors sell roasted pupae that are flavoured with sugar and soy sauce.

▲ Italian silk was woven into heavy brocades and patterned velvets.

Silk in Europe

Arab invaders conquered Persia around AD 600. This gave them control of the silk industry there. The art of making silk spread throughout the Arab world, across North Africa and into Spain and Sicily, an island off the coast of Italy.

New ideas

People invented new types of silk cloth and new machines to weave patterns into silk instead of doing all this work by hand. Still, many silk producers in Europe and later in America depended on **raw silk** from Asia.

throughout Europe. The French bought silk from Italy until the king of France decided to develop his own silk industry. The city of Lyon became the centre of the French silk trade. King James I (1566–1625) tried to start an English silk industry in the grounds of what is now Buckingham Palace. But his project was a failure because the mulberry trees did not grow.

Silk in America

King James did succeed in spreading sericulture to America. In 1619, the first silkworms arrived there. However, the silk industry did not really take off in America until after the **Industrial Revolution**. Unlike the **cottage industries** of Asia, silk production in America was based in large factories. A city called Paterson made so much of this luxury fabric, it became known as "Silk City".

◀ Queen Victoria wore a white silk wedding dress in 1840. White silk wedding gowns are still very popular today.

Silk in fashion

▲ A French silk weaver invented a loom that could be programmed to produce complicated patterns. The program was on punch cards, which you can see in a stack on the right side of the loom.

The way people unwind **cocoons** to produce raw silk thread has stayed mostly the same for the past 5,000 years. However, what people do with **raw silk** keeps changing. Throughout history, people have invented new ways to weave and colour silk to make many different kinds of fabric.

Here are some of the more common silk fabrics:

- *Brocade* is a thick, heavy silk fabric with a raised design or pattern on one side.
- *Damask* is similar to brocade, but it is flatter and reversible.
- *Chiffon* is so thin, you can see right through it.
- *Crepe* is a light, soft, thin silk fabric that looks all crinkly and wrinkly.
- *Organdie* (sometimes also called organza) is a thin, stiff silk fabric.
- *Satin* is very shiny on only one side. Some satins are so smooth, they actually feel slippery.
- *Taffeta* is silk treated with chemicals to make it stiff and crisp.
- *Shantung* is silk made from broken cocoons. It has a rough, bumpy feel from its uneven **fibres**.
- *Velvet* is soft and furry on one side, and smooth on the other.

Silk blends

Raw silk is also woven together with other natural fibres, such as cotton or wool. These blended fabrics have the best qualities of each fibre. You can tell what your clothes are made from by looking at the labels.

▼ **Raw silk is usually white or light beige.**

23

Wallace Hume Carothers (1869-1937)

Wallace Hume Carothers (below) was born in Iowa, USA. He taught at the University of Illinois for a few years but then went to work for the DuPont Company in 1928. They wanted him to help create a synthetic replacement for silk. Nylon was the result. He also invented neoprene, a synthetic rubber.

▶ Nylon stockings were just as thin as silk, but much less expensive.

Silk stockings

Silk stockings were first made in the 1500s. Men and women wore them. Before that, stockings were made from other natural fibres, especially wool. But silk felt nicer next to the skin because it wasn't scratchy like wool.

Although some women still choose silk stockings today, there are other much less expensive options. Scientists at the DuPont Company in the United States experimented with chemicals, and discovered ways to make **synthetic**, silk-like fabrics, including **nylon**. Nylon stockings became a fashion craze in the 1940s.

Fashion at a cost?

Silk is a great choice for fashion designers and people who enjoy its look and feel. It is environmentally friendly, too. The United Nations named 2009 the Year of Natural Fibres to remind people worldwide of the benefits of natural fibres such as silk.

Silk farms do not cause pollution. Silk **cottage industries** provide much needed income for poor families who live in the countryside of India and other parts of Asia. However, human rights organizations are concerned that children are being used like slaves in India's silk industry. According to some reports, children under the age of 14 work 80 hours or more each week in bad and dangerous conditions.

▼ These racks of cocoons are on a silk farm in Vietnam.

Strange silks

▲ Silk can be used as an ingredient in make-up like this.

Today there are many new fabrics with the "look and feel" of silk. But even if silk is on its way out as a fashion fabric, it has many other uses. Long ago in Asia, people used silk to make soft body armour. Silk parachutes brought soldiers safely to the ground during World War I. Doctors used silk to stitch wounds closed. Some fishing lines are made of silk. Silk is still used to make bicycle tyres. Silk is even ground into a soft powder and used in make-up.

Super silk

Silk is strong, but the **fibre** that makes a spider's web is even stronger. So far, no one has been able to raise spiders for their super strong silk. One problem is that spiders cannot live close together, like silkworms. They will fight and even eat each other.

Since spiders cannot be **domesticated**, scientists are looking for other ways to get even stronger silk from domesticated silkworms. They may have succeeded! They discovered that silkworms can make tougher or more elastic fibres. It depends on how fast they're forced to spin. These super silks could make better medical supplies, seat belts, and maybe even an improved bullet-proof vest.

▼ The fibre of a spider's web is about a tenth as thick as silk, and still stronger and stretchier than any human-made fibre.

Timeline

(These dates are often approximations.)

2700 BC	**2697–2597 BC**
Silk is discovered in China.	The first emperor of China – the "Yellow Emperor" – reigns.

3000 BC →

AD 100 ← 0

AD 300
Sericulture spreads from China to India, Korea, and Persia (present-day Iran).

AD 200 → AD 300 →

AD 900 ← AD 800

1148
Italian silk industry is started at Palermo (Sicily) using Greek silk workers. Italy becomes a major silk producer and sells silk throughout Europe.

1000 1100 →

1619	**1609**
The first silkworms arrive in America.	King James I tries to start an English silk industry in the grounds of what is now Buckingham Palace. His project is a failure.

1700 ← 1600

1800s	**1914–1918**	**1935**
The **Industrial Revolution** modernizes silk production and the American silk industry takes off, especially in "Silk City" Paterson, New Jersey.	Silk parachutes are used during World War I.	DuPont scientists invent **nylon**.

1800 1900 →

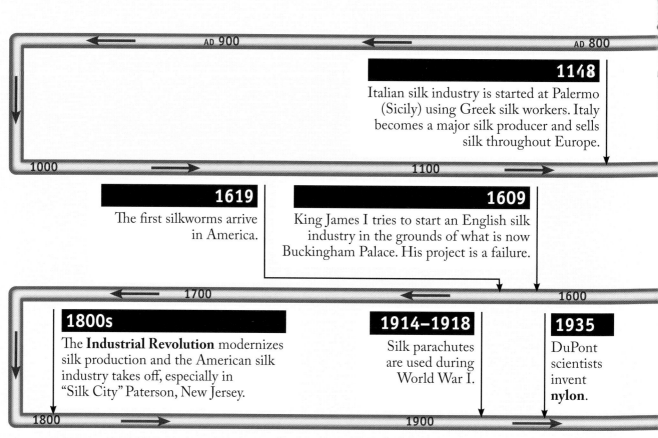

28   ∿∿∿   This symbol shows where there is a change of scale in the timeline, or where a long period of time with no noted events has been left out.

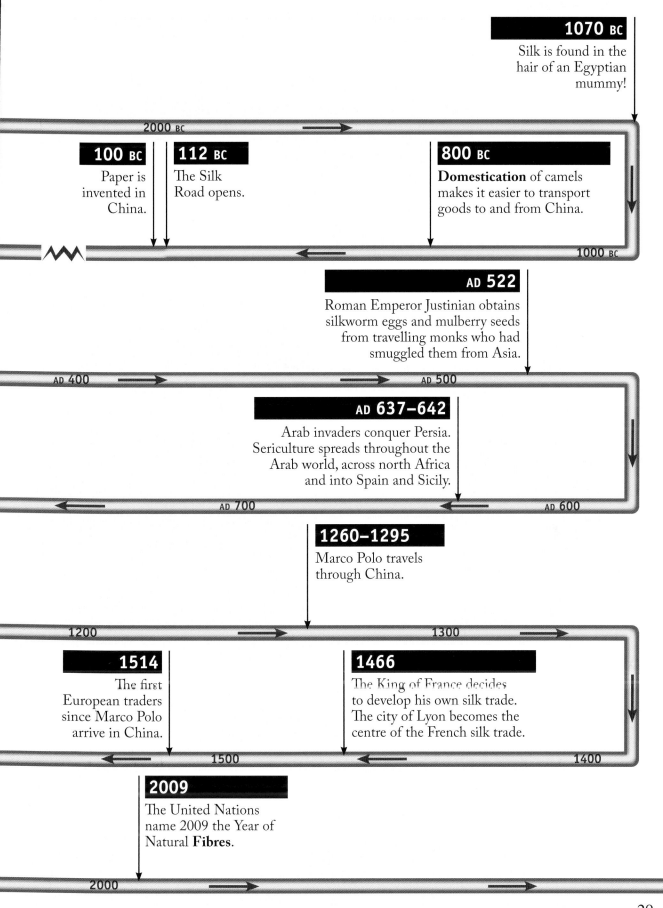

1070 BC

Silk is found in the hair of an Egyptian mummy!

2000 BC

100 BC

Paper is invented in China.

112 BC

The Silk Road opens.

800 BC

Domestication of camels makes it easier to transport goods to and from China.

1000 BC

AD 522

Roman Emperor Justinian obtains silkworm eggs and mulberry seeds from travelling monks who had smuggled them from Asia.

AD 400

AD 500

AD 637–642

Arab invaders conquer Persia. Sericulture spreads throughout the Arab world, across north Africa and into Spain and Sicily.

AD 700

AD 600

1260–1295

Marco Polo travels through China.

1200

1300

1514

The first European traders since Marco Polo arrive in China.

1466

The King of France decides to develop his own silk trade. The city of Lyon becomes the centre of the French silk trade.

1500

1400

2009

The United Nations name 2009 the Year of Natural **Fibres**.

2000

Glossary

caravan group of traders, with their camels, travelling together for safety

cocoon what a caterpillar makes to surround and protect itself while it changes into a moth

cottage industry work done by people at home using their own equipment

domesticate train an animal to live with people. Farm animals, horses, and dogs are examples of domesticated animals.

embroider sew a pattern into a fabric for decoration

fibre long, thin thread of a material

glands body parts that use what is in the blood to make something new

Industrial Revolution time period from about 1750 to 1850, when people first began using fuel-powered machines to do work on a large scale

legend ancient story that is told over many generations

loom machine for weaving cloth from thread

luxury something expensive or hard to get that people want, but can do without

nylon a fabric made using chemical fibres. Nylon is also used to make brushes and containers.

prism piece of glass cut in the shape of a long triangle that reflects light in a special way to create a rainbow of colours

pupa (plural: **pupae**) stage of an insect's life cycle when it is inside its cocoon

raw silk silk thread or fabric in its natural state before it is dyed

Roman Empire large empire that controlled land and people from the Middle East to southern Britain for hundreds of years

sari long rectangle of cloth worn as a garment by women in India. A sari is wrapped around the waist and draped over one shoulder.

scholar adult student or person respected for their knowledge on a particular subject

sericulture art and science of breeding silkworms to make and sell silk

spool cylinder around which thread is wound. Many people keep spools of thread in a sewing kit.

synthetic substance that is human-made (from chemicals), not found in nature

taxes money paid to the people who run the country

Find out more

Books

The Adventures of Marco Polo (Graphic History), Roger Smalley (Raintree, 2011)

The Biography of Silk (How Did That Get Here?), Carrie Gleason (Crabtree, 2007)

Marco Polo's Travels on Asia's Silk Road (Great Journeys), Cath Senker (Heinemann Library, 2007)

Website

www.historyforkids.org/learn/clothing/silk.htm
Learn more about silk and how it is made.

Places to visit

Paradise Mill
Old Park Lane
Macclesfield
Cheshire SK11 2TJ
www.macclesfield.silk.museum/visit-our-museums

Silk Heritage Museum
The Heritage Centre
Roe Street
Macclesfield
Cheshire SK11 6UT
www.macclesfield.silk.museum/visit-our-museums

National Museum of Costume
Shambellie House
New Abbey
Dumfries DG2 8HQ
Scotland
www.nms.ac.uk/our_museums/museum_of_costume.aspx